BIOGRAPHY FROM
ANCIENT CIVILIZATIONS
LEGENDS, FOLKLORE, AND STORIES OF ANCIENT WORLDS

The Life and Times of

HOMER

Mitchell Lane
PUBLISHERS

P.O. Box 196
Hockessin, Delaware 19707

Titles in the Series

The Life and Times of

BIOGRAPHY FROM
ANCIENT CIVILIZATIONS
LEGENDS, FOLKLORE, AND STORIES OF ANCIENT WORLDS

The Life and Times of

HOMER

by Kathleen Tracy

Printing   4   5   6   7   8

Library of Congress Cataloging-in-Publication Data
Tracy, Kathleen.
The life and times of Homer / Kathleen Tracy.
        p. cm. — (Biography from ancient civilizations)
    Includes bibliographical references (p.) and index.
    Contents: A myth comes alive —Piecing together a life—The rise of a legend—Iliad and Odyssey—Homer's legacy.
    ISBN 1-58415-260-5 (lib. bdg.)
    1. Homer—Juvenile literature. 2. Epic poetry, Greek—History and criticism—Juvenile literature. 3. Trojan War—Literature and the war—Juvenile literature. 4. Mythology, Greek, in literature—Juvenile literature. 5. Poets, Greek—Biography—Juvenile literature. 6. Civilization, Homeric—Juvenile literature. [1. Homer. 2. Epic poetry. 3. Trojan War. 4. Mythology, Greek. 5. Poets, Greek. 6. Greece—Civilization—To 146 B.C.] I. Title. II. Series.
PA4037.T675 2004
883'.01—dc22   2003024128
ISBN-13: 9781584152606

J-B
HOMER
370-0385

ABOUT THE AUTHOR: Kathleen Tracy has been a journalist for over twenty years. Her writing has been featured in magazines including *The Toronto Star*'s "Star Week," *A&E Biography* magazine, *KidScreen* and *TV Times*. She is also the author of numerous biographies including *The Boy Who Would Be King* (Dutton), *Jerry Seinfeld—The Entire Domain* (Carol Publishing) and *Don Imus—America's Cowboy* (Carroll & Graf), and *The Complete Idoit's Guide to Portrait Photography* for Alpha Books.

PHOTO CREDITS: Cover, title page, half-title page, pp. 6, 14, 23 28, 36—Superstock; pp. 8, 10, 16, 20, 33, 40—Hulton Archive/Getty Images; pp. 25, 32—CORBIS; pp. 24, 30 picture history.

PUBLISHER'S NOTE: This story is based on the author's extensive research, which she believes to be accurate. Documentation of such research is contained on page 47.
    The internet sites referenced herein were active as of the publication date. Due to the fleeting nature of some web sites, we cannot guarantee they will all be active when you are reading this book.

PLB2,4

BIOGRAPHY FROM ANCIENT CIVILIZATIONS

LEGENDS, FOLKLORE, AND STORIES OF ANCIENT WORLDS

The Life and Times of

HOMER

*For Your Information

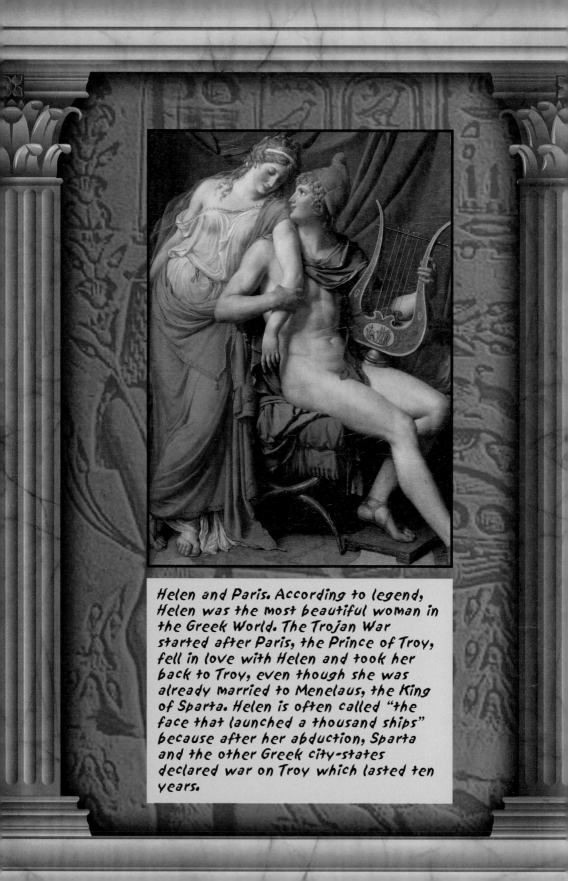

Helen and Paris. According to legend, Helen was the most beautiful woman in the Greek World. The Trojan War started after Paris, the Prince of Troy, fell in love with Helen and took her back to Troy, even though she was already married to Menelaus, the King of Sparta. Helen is often called "the face that launched a thousand ships" because after her abduction, Sparta and the other Greek city-states declared war on Troy which lasted ten years.

CHAPTER
ONE

A MYTH COMES ALIVE

Over three thousand years ago the bustling city of Troy was famous. Completely surrounded by a thick wall, the city was impenetrable to attack. Only one huge set of gates allowed access in or out of the city. For hundreds of years, the walls had kept the city safe from enemies looking to steal its great wealth.

But the city's peace was shattered after Paris, Prince of Troy, stole Helen, the wife of Menelaus, King of Sparta. Furious, Menelaus and his brother Agamemnon joined with other Greeks and declared war on Troy. For ten years the battles raged as the Greeks tried to storm the city, but the mighty wall of Troy kept the invaders out and its citizens safe.

One morning the citizens of Troy, known as the Trojans, awoke and were stunned to see that the Greek soldiers had disbanded their camp and set sail for home. Standing outside the gates to the city was a gigantic wooden horse, which they were told was a gift to the goddess Athena from the defeated Greeks. Deliriously happy that the war was finally over, the gates to the

In order to defeat their enemies, the Greeks tricked the Trojans into accepting the gift of a giant wooden horse, which was filled with Greek soldiers.

city were opened and the horse was pulled into the center of town.

Little did they suspect that the wooden horse was a trap. Silently cramped inside was a group of Greek soldiers, including the hero Odysseus, who had devised the plan. Knowing they would never be able to penetrate the wall of Troy, Odysseus decided the only way to get inside was by trickery. He convinced the other Greeks to build a wooden horse big enough to hold him and a group of soldiers. Once the soldiers were inside, the horse would be left at the gates of Troy while the rest of the Greek troops would set sail, pretending to return to Greece.

The Trojans were eager to see the unique peace offering up close. King Priam's daughter Cassandra, however, warned her father that bringing in the horse would lead to the destruction of Troy. The god Apollo had given Cassandra the ability to see the future as a special gift. However, when she refused his romantic advances, he added a curse to the gift: no one would believe her prophecies. Cassandra watched in despair as the gates were opened and the rejoicing Trojans hauled the horse into the center of town and began celebrating. She knew it was only a matter of time before their destruction and went to pray at the altar of the goddess Athena.

The Trojans feasted, drank, and danced until late into the night. Finally, one by one, they passed out from either exhaustion or drunkenness. Hearing the quiet around them, Odysseus and the others opened the trapdoor and jumped down to the ground. There was a full moon overhead, so they could see everything around them. They immediately killed the sentries and flung the gates open, allowing in the rest of the Greek soldiers, who had sailed back and had been hiding nearby.

Caught completely off guard, the Trojans were slaughtered. Nearly every male in the city was killed, including the children of Troy's heroes. The swords of the Greeks ran red with blood and the skies above the city were filled with shrieks of terror and cries of agony. Menelaus had vowed to kill Helen for her betrayal, but when he finally confronted her, he once again was so taken with her beauty, he spared her life and they left Troy together.

After the Greeks had plundered Troy's wealth, they set fire to the city. Troy was burned to the ground. So complete was the destruction that in later years nobody knew if the city of Troy had ever really existed. And we might have never known if it

Self-taught German archaeologist Heinrich Schliemann grew up fascinated by stories of the Trojan War and was determined to prove the city had really existed.

weren't for two men named Frank Calvert and Heinrich Schliemann.

While still a child, Schliemann became obsessed with discovering Troy.[1] His father gave him a book of stories about the beautiful city known for its prosperity and beauty—and its impenetrable wall. But it wasn't until 1868, when he was 46 years old and financially secure, that Schliemann took up archaeology. The few scientists and scholars who believed Troy had been a real place thought it would have most likely been located in Turkey on a hill known as Bunarbashi, which was a few miles inland from the Aegean Sea.

While traveling the area, Schliemann visited a mound in Turkey called Hisarlik. There he met Frank Calvert, a British archaeologist who had spent fifteen years excavating in the region. Calvert had found enough tantalizing evidence to be convinced he had found the true location of Troy. In order to have unrestricted access to the site, Calvert bought part of the land from the Turkish government. But not everyone agreed with Calvert's analysis. The British Museum, which was funding his digs, was skeptical and didn't want to give him any more money. By the time Schliemann arrived, Calvert was desperate for funds, so he confided in Schliemann and revealed his discoveries. He explained why he believed Troy lay buried beneath Hisarlik.[2]

Schliemann returned to Paris, France, and spent the next six months immersing himself on the history of Troy. He kept in touch with Calvert, asking his opinion about where the best place to dig would be and what equipment would be needed for the excavation. Two years later, Schliemann returned to Hisarlik and began excavating using a permit Frank Calvert had obtained for him and employing members of Calvert's crew. At the time, Schliemann's experience as an archaeologist consisted of two excavations totaling less than five days.

Over the next three years Schliemann found evidence that several cities had been built on the site of Hisarlik over the millennia. Near the bottom of the excavation, at about 53 feet down, were the ruins of an ancient city with massive walls, well-built houses, and treasures of gold and silver. There was no doubt in his mind that this was the ancient city of Troy.

Since then, over one hundred excavations have been made at the site. Archaeologists have discovered ten different settlements on the site where Troy stood, beginning as far back as 2300 B.C., with each new city built on the ruins of the one before it. Today, most scholars believe the seventh city was the legendary city of Troy. Scientists have uncovered evidence that the city was indeed destroyed by a huge fire that consumed the structures inside and outside the fortification walls. Human skeletons that appear to have been left lying in the open have also been found, indicating some type of massacre.

The reason Calvert succeeded where others had failed was because he relied on the writings of an ancient Greek poet named Homer. Homer's *Iliad* tells the story of the Trojan War, and Calvert used descriptions given in the verses as a guide; they directed him to the mound at Hisarlik. Without Calvert, the true power and importance of Homer's classic masterpiece might have never been known. Once it became clear that the Trojan War had been an actual event, scholars took a fresh look at Homer, the poet who kept alive the heroics that occurred during one of the most significant wars in the history of Greece, and which in turn paved the way for the rise of classical Greek civilization.

The Olympians

The Olympians were the twelve gods who the Greeks believed ruled their world and controlled everything from war to the weather. To the Greeks, humans were at the constant mercy of the Olympians, who they believed enjoyed creating havoc. The Olympians came to power after overthrowing the elder gods, known as the Titans, and were named after Mount Olympus, where they were believed to live. All the Olympians were related in some way.

- Zeus (zoos): After defeating his father Cronus, Zeus and his two brothers, Poseidon and Hades, drew straws to see who would be the supreme ruler of all the gods. Zeus won and became master of the sky.
- Hera (HEER uh): Zeus' wife and sister, Hera was jealous of her husband's romances with mortal women and often punished the women severely.
- Poseidon (puh SY duhn): God of the ocean. His weapon was the trident, which could shake the earth and destroy any object. Only his brother Zeus was stronger.

- Hades (HAY deez): When drawing straws for control of the world, Hades came up with the worst pick and became the god of the underworld, ruling over the dead. However, because he lived underground, he was also the god of wealth—all the precious metals, such as gold, are found underground.
- Hestia (HEHS tee uh): Goddess of the hearth. It is believed her place on Olympus was later taken by Dionysus, the god of wine and ecstasy.
- Ares (AIR eez): The son of Zeus and Hera, Ares was the god of war.
- Athena (uh THEE nuh): Zeus' daughter Athena sprang fully formed from his head—complete with a suit of armor. She was the goddess of agriculture and invented the bridle, thus allowing humans to tame horses.
- Apollo (uh POL oh): The son of Zeus and Leto, Apollo had a twin sister, Artemis. He was the god of music and played a golden lyre, a kind of harp. He taught mortals medicine, but his most important job was to use his chariot to drive the sun across the sky.
- Artemis (AHR tuh mihs): Apollo's twin sister, Artemis was known for her hunting skills.
- Aphrodite (af roh DY tee): Daughter of Zeus and goddess of love, Aphrodite was romantically involved with Ares.
- Hermes (HUR meez): The son of Zeus, Hermes was Zeus' messenger.
- Hephaestus (hih FEHS tuhs): The son of Zeus and Hera, Hephaestus was the only god considered ugly. He was also lame, having suffered broken legs after birth. He was the god of fire and the husband of Aphrodite.

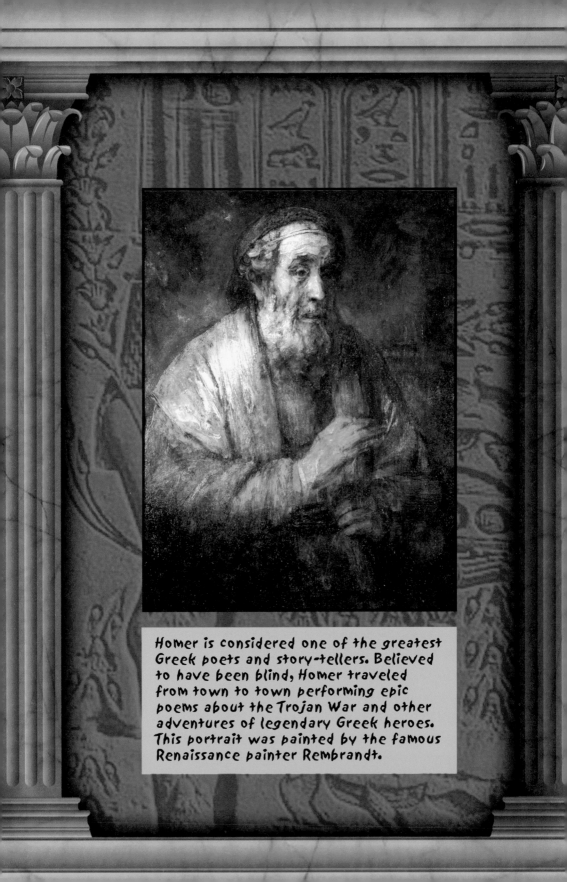

Homer is considered one of the greatest
Greek poets and story-tellers. Believed
to have been blind, Homer traveled
from town to town performing epic
poems about the Trojan War and other
adventures of legendary Greek heroes.
This portrait was painted by the famous
Renaissance painter Rembrandt.

CHAPTER
TWO

PIECING TOGETHER A LIFE

Despite all our research and modern technology, much of Homer's life remains a muddled mystery. Because he lived during a time when people were just beginning to use the written word, much of our information about him comes to us either through tradition or inference from reading the works of other ancient Greeks. Because of this, there is scholarly disagreement about the very basics of Homer's life, including where and when he was born. While some think Homer was born as recently as 700 B.C., most believe it was closer to 850 B.C., based on the writings of Herodotus, the man called the world's first historian.

Homer's family history is equally murky. It's hard to know who to believe, but the most intriguing family history comes from the time of the Roman emperor Hadrian, who lived shortly after the time of Christ. According to the account, the emperor asked a *pythia*, or priestess, to tell him about Homer. She told him the poet had been born in Ithaca and that his father was Telemachus and his mother was Epicasta, the daughter of

Telemachus was the son of the Greek hero Odysseus. Most historians discount the story that Telemachus was Homer's father.

Nestor. What's interesting about this account is that Telemachus was the son of Odysseus, and Nestor, who would be Homer's grandfather, was one of the Greeks said to have fought in the war against Troy. Obviously, this family tree would explain Homer's fascination with the Trojan War, as well as with Odysseus, who is immortalized in *The Odyssey*. However, many scholars prefer to trust the writings of Herodotus, the Greek historian who lived from approximately 485 to 425 B.C. and who is credited with writing *The Life of Homer.*

According to Herodotus, Homer's grandfather was Menapolus. He fathered a daughter named Critheis, who was orphaned at a young age. She became pregnant and gave birth to a son she named Melesigenes because he was born near the

Meles River in Smyrna, located in modern-day Turkey. Most scholars agree with this account.

Herodotus says that Critheis was hired by a literature and music teacher named Phemius to manage his household. Eventually he asked her to marry him and adopted her son. Melesigenes began attending Phemius's school and quickly proved himself to be a superior student. When Phemius died, he left his property to Melesigenes. Critheis died a short time later, and Melesigenes supported himself by running his stepfather's school.

One day a traveler named Mentes, who was as intelligent as Melesigenes, came to Smyrna. Mentes convinced his new friend to close the school and join him on his travels, encouraging the young man to see the world and offering to pay his way. Having no family to tie him to Smyrna, Melesigenes agreed, and they sailed to Ithaca, an island off the northwest coast of Greece and the traditional home of the Greek hero Odysseus. However, Melesigenes began having trouble with his eyes, so Mentes took him to stay with his friend Mentor before sailing away on his next adventure. Mentor entertained his guest with stories about the local hero Odysseus, and when Melesigenes returned home to Smyrna, he immersed himself in the study of poetry.

At some point, Melesigenes' eye trouble rendered him blind. At least, that is the common belief. Whether he was truly blind or perhaps just suffered from very bad eyesight is unknown. In any event, now penniless, he traveled to Cyme, where he began reciting verses. It was there that he was given the name Homer because that's what the locals called all blind men.

Although his poetry was appreciated by the people of Cyme, the city elders refused to grant his request to be paid a fee for his poetry performances. According to Herodotus, one man "observed that if they were to feed Homers, the city would be encumbered with a multitude of useless people."[1] The poverty-stricken Homer moved on, continuing to live a nomadic life.

Homer traveled to Larissa and then to Phocaea, where he took a room with a man named Thestorides, who paid Homer to write poems. What Homer didn't know was that Thestorides was passing the poems off as his own and getting paid handsomely for reciting them. Not only did Thestorides not give Homer any credit, he eventually turned Homer out. Herodotus says when Homer finally moved on, he said: "O Thestorides, of the many things hidden from the knowledge of man, nothing is more unintelligible than the human heart."[2]

But Homer's fortunes were about to change and his days of poverty would soon be over.

Ancient Greece

Greece was first settled about 57,000 years ago. For a long time, not many people lived there. Unlike Egypt across the Mediterranean Sea, Greece did not have good soil for raising crops, so it was a hard place to live comfortably. But through the ages, more and more people adapted to the land, and by 1600 B.C. Greek culture and trade with nearby countries such as Phoenicia and Egypt were well established. This was during a period scholars call the Bronze Age, because during this time people used weapons and tools made from bronze.

Sometime around 1200 B.C., Greece went through a troubled time known as the Greek Dark Ages. Crime was rampant and many of the ornate Greek palaces were destroyed. Scholars can only speculate about the reasons, but it is suspected that the economy became depressed. With not enough jobs or food available, people found themselves living in poverty. For the next several hundred years there was little order in Greece, and people were forced to fend for themselves.

With no centralized rulers, Greece was an easy target for invaders. Peoples from the north came to live in Greece and took over some of the Greek cities. The Greeks called these invaders Dorians, while the native Greeks were called Ionians. Many Ionians left Greece during the Dark Ages and settled in what is now Turkey. In fact, so many Greeks moved there that the area became known as Ionia.

Those Ionians who stayed were forced to adapt in order to survive. They learned how to make tools and weapons out of iron, which was a big advance because iron is stronger than bronze and less expensive to obtain. Even poor people could use iron. The Iron Age helped the Greeks rebuild their civilization. It brought an end to the Dark Ages and ushered in an era scholars call Greece's Archaic Period.

During this time, which lasted from approximately 900 to 500 B.C., the population of Greece grew, as did the power of city-states such as Sparta and Athens, which ruled their surrounding area. More money led to increased trading, especially with the Phoenicians, who had developed a form of writing that the Greeks adopted. This development was a pivotal point in the history of Greece because stories had previously been passed down only through oral tradition. Now they could be written down.

Hesiod was another famous Greek poet who most scholars believe rose to fame after Homer's death. But some legends suggest that Hesiod and Homer were contemporary rivals who once had a contest to see whose poetry was better.

CHAPTER
THREE

THE RISE OF A LEGEND

With no money to his name and his poetry being appropriated by others, Homer's future looked bleak. Finally some merchants from Chios told Homer about Thestorides' deception, prompting Homer to set sail for the island, located off the coast of what is now Turkey. In a tiny spot named Pithys, Homer met a goat herder named Glaucus. After hearing Homer's misfortunes, Glaucus invited Homer to stay with him and introduced him to his master, who was so impressed with Homer's intelligence and poetic abilities that he hired him to tutor his children.[1]

Eventually Thestorides was revealed as a fraud and forced to leave the island. Homer found personal and financial success as a teacher and was able to establish his own school in the town of Chios, located on the eastern coast near the Aegean Sea. He taught poetry there and became a wealthy man. Once he was settled, he married and had two children. Through his poetry, Homer became a local celebrity, and soon people were urging him to expand his reputation by taking his poetry on the road.

Homer sailed to the nearby island of Samos and was invited to participate in a festival there. His poetry was warmly received, and he earned money for his performance. He also made house calls, going to the homes of wealthy citizens and giving private performances. But most of the time he would recite his poetry in front of a group who gathered in anticipation at the agora, or town meeting place. Like many other storytellers, or bards, Homer sang stories about the Trojan War and its Greek heroes. The songs, which were his poems set to music and sung accompanied by a lyre, were so long it would take several evenings to finish them. The people who listened to Homer never tired of hearing about the heroic deeds of their ancestors, and the poems instilled a kind of national pride that had never been part of the Ionian culture.

Homer was considered by those who heard him to be the best living poet—much to the frustration of Hesiod, another poet who scholars believe lived around the time of Homer. Hesiod was born in Boeotia in central Greece and worked as a farmer. Like Homer, few definitive facts are known about his life, but his two great epics, *Works and Days* and *Theogony*, are still studied today. While Homer concentrated on heroic deeds of the past, Hesiod dealt more with the realities of daily Greek living. *Works and Days* describes the rural life of Greek farmers, while *Theogony* is a genealogy of the gods, a retelling of the creation myth and an essay on the ages of mankind—the Golden Age, which was ruled by Cronus and was a time of peace; the Silver Age, presided over by Zeus, which was less ideal than the Golden Age but was still a prosperous time; the Bronze Age, a period of strife during the Greek Dark Ages; the Heroic Age of the Trojan War; and finally the Iron Age, Hesiod's present, during which he believed justice and holiness had vanished (a view similar to those held by some

Homer traveled throughout Greece to recite his poetry. Epics such as The Iliad
were so long it would take him several evenings to finish.

modern social commentators). Between them, Homer and
Hesiod would preserve the myths of the classical Greek gods for
eons.

.According to one famous account, Hesiod and Homer, who
were said to be rivals, met at Chalcis in Euboea and entered into
a competition held by the king of Euboea. The contest consisted
of the poets' asking each other questions; they were judged on
the intelligence and wittiness of the answers. Surprisingly,
Hesiod is said to have won because of his relentless questions.
But the contest did little to affect Homer's reputation, and after-
ward he continued traveling and reciting his poems. Gorgus, the
son of King Midas, was among those who heard Homer's epics.
He asked the poet to compose a epitaph for the tomb of his
father. On the tomb was a bronze sculpture of a woman grieving

Delphi was one of the holiest places in the ancient world and was considered to be the center of the world by the Greeks.

over the death of Midas. According to Herodotus's *The Life of Homer*, the poet wrote:

> *I am a maiden of bronze and sit upon the tomb of Midas. While water flows, and tall trees put forth leaves, and rivers swell, and the sea breaks on the shore; while the sun rises and shines and the bright moon also, ever remaining on this mournful tomb I tell the passer-by that Midas here lies buried.*[2]

After stopping in Delphi, where he made an offering to Apollo, it is believed that Homer composed the *Odyssey*, an epic that contains 12,110 verses. Feeling ever more confident, Homer eventually headed toward Athens, hoping to capture the imagination of the great city-state. He was warmly welcomed by the king, Medon. It is believed that Homer adjusted some of the verses to play up the Athenian role in the Trojan War to please

This painting by Claude Lorrain, called "Aeneas at Delos," depicts how the Greek island of Delos might have looked during Homer's time. According to Greek mythology, Aeneas survived Troy's downfall and later traveled to Italy where his descendants founded Rome.

the locals. From there he visited Corinth and Argos. Everywhere he went he performed his verses and was lavished with gifts and money. In Argos a statue with the following inscription was erected in his honor:

This is divine Homer who by his sweet-voiced art honored all proud Hellas, but especially the Argives who threw down the god-built walls of Troy to avenge rich-haired Helen. For this cause the people of a great city set his statue here and serve him with the honors of the deathless gods.

While on the isle of Delos, the local Ionians made him an honorary citizen of all the city-states, possibly the greatest honor Homer had ever received. It showed how through his stories he had united all the peoples of the area and made them think of themselves not just as Athenians or Argives but as Greeks.

Despite his notoriety, had Homer lived just a few decades earlier, he might have disappeared from history in the years that followed, like so many other poets before him. In all, it is believed that Homer sang ten epic poems about the Trojan War but only two survived. It is doubtful Homer had been the first to tell the stories contained in *The Iliad* and *The Odyssey*, but he is credited with being a particularly powerful storyteller and was the one who took the time to write them down first. Once written, he was able to perfect each one and make them the masterpieces we consider them today.

Ancient Greek Fashion

Like people in modern times, the ancient Greeks enjoyed fashion. However, they were much less self-conscious about their bodies than we are in today's society. They found the human form pleasing and wore styles meant to be flattering. That said, Greek clothing was very simple. Men and women wore linen in the summer and wool in the winter.

The clothing styles of men and women during the Archaic and Classical periods were very similar. There were two basic garments. The primary article of clothing was called a chiton, which was made from a large rectangular piece of cloth that was draped to form a loose-fitting tunic. Chitons were sleeveless, in order to show off a person's arms, and the Greeks liked dying their clothes an assortment of colors. Some chitons were decorated with embroidery of silver or gold thread.

The chiton was worn a number of ways. It could be pinned at the shoulders and tied at the waist or pinned on the left shoulder only, leaving the right shoulder and arm free. Up until the fifth century B.C., all Greek men wore a full-length chiton, but then the fashion changed and the garments became knee-length. Older males also wore long draped mantles either alone or over their chiton.

The himation was the other basic garment. It was a wool cloak that was worn when it was cold. It could also double as a blanket for soldiers out in the field. Shoes were optional. Although leather sandals were available, many Greeks went barefoot their whole lives.

Women's chitons were draped in numerous ways and were also worn with mantles and accessorized with jewelry. Hair was worn long and was often held in place with a headband or scarf. But if a woman was mourning the death of a loved one, she had her hair cut off as a symbol of her grief.

Before Achilles left to fight in the Trojan War, his mother Thetis gave him a magical suit of armor and two immortal horses. Achilles is considered one of the greatest and bravest of all Greek heroes.

CHAPTER

FOUR

ILIAD AND ODYSSEY

In all probability, the war between the Trojans and the Greeks occurred around 1200 B.C. and was likely caused by a trade dispute over who would control the Dardanelles, a narrow strait in northwestern Turkey that connects the Aegean Sea with the Marmara Sea and separates Europe and the mainland of Asia. Throughout history, the strait has been important both tactically and economically. However, the *Iliad* tells a more compelling story of the Trojan War. The action related in the *Iliad* takes place over a four-day period in the pivotal tenth year of the conflict. The poem is presented in twenty-four books. It centers on the Greek hero Achilles and the tragedy that befalls the Greek soldiers as a result of his falling out with Agamemnon.

Sing, O goddess, the anger of Achilles son of Peleus, that brought countless ills upon the Achaeans. Many a brave soul did it send hurrying down to Hades, and many a hero did it yield a prey to dogs and vultures, for so were the counsels of Zeus fulfilled from the day on which the son of Atreus, king of men, and great Achilles, first fell out with one another.[1]

At Thetis' wedding to Peleus, goddess of love Aphrodite promised Paris the love of the most beautiful woman in the world. Paris' obsession with Helen would lead to the Trojan War.

However, it wasn't Achilles who caused the war. That dubious honor went to a young Trojan prince named Paris. As usual, as told by Homer, the gods also had their hands in the action. The seeds of the war were unwittingly sown by Peleus and Thetis when they got married and neglected to invite the goddess of discord, Eris. Irate, she crashed the wedding reception and left behind a golden apple, which she said belonged to the most beautiful goddess. Immediately, three different goddesses—Hera, Athena, and Aphrodite—reached for the apple. To settle the dispute, Zeus decided that Paris, considered by many to be the most handsome man in the world, would be the judge to decide who should get the apple.

All three goddesses promised Paris a gift in hopes of swaying him. Hera promised him power, Athena promised him victory in battle, and Aphrodite promised him the love of the most beautiful woman in the world. Paris chose Aphrodite, and she kept her promise. Unfortunately, the most beautiful woman in the world was Helen, who was already married to Menelaus, the king of Sparta. Paris was determined to claim his prize, so he set sail for Sparta, despite the warnings of others, including the prophet Cassandra, that he would cause the fall of Troy if he did not leave Helen alone.

Once he reached Sparta, an unaware Menelaus welcomed Paris as a royal guest. When Menelaus left Sparta to attend a funeral, Paris made his move and abducted Helen. He took a lot of Menelaus's money as well. It is suggested that Helen may have left with Paris willingly. In either event, once they got to Troy, Paris and Helen were married.

Menelaus, of course, was outraged. His brother, the powerful Agamemnon, called on all the kings of Greece to join with him to defend Helen's honor and bring her home. The hero Achilles was also recruited, because the seer Calchas had prophesied that Greece could not win without him. Once the soldiers were assembled, however, they were stuck at port because there was no wind. Once again, Calchas intervened. He told Agamemnon that his daughter Iphigenia would have to be sacrificed before the fleet could set sail. Agamemnon complied, and soon after the winds picked up and the Greek ships set sail. Once in Troy, Menelaus appealed to the Trojan king Priam to return Helen and the money, but he refused. The war ensued. It would take ten years and the clever deception of a hollowed-out wooden horse for the Greeks to defeat Troy.

According to The Iliad, *Agamemnon was forced to sacrifice his daughter Iphigenia before the gods sent favorable winds allowing his fleet to sail to Troy. Ten years later when he returned from the war, Agamemnon was killed by his wife to revenge Iphigenia's death.*

Although they won, not all the Greeks had happy endings, such as Agamemnon, who returned home only to be murdered by his wife for having sacrificed their daughter. Meanwhile, it took Odysseus ten years after the end of the war to get home. His long, drawn-out journey was the subject of Homer's other epic, *The Odyssey*. While *The Iliad* is a tragedy in every sense, *The Odyssey* has lighter moments interspersed with the drama.

Penelope was Odysseus' devoted wife. Once the Trojan War was over, it took Odysseus another ten years to make his way home. His adventures are recounted in Homer's The Odyssey.

The Odyssey begins ten years after the end of the Trojan War and takes place over the course of forty days. All the Greek heroes but one have returned home. Odysseus is trapped on the island of Ogygia with the goddess Calypso, who has fallen in love with him and refuses to let him leave. His absence back home has left his kingdom in chaos, as would-be suitors descend on his wife Penelope. His son, Telemachus, who was an infant when Odysseus left, is now a young man, but he feels helpless to protect his mother or defend his father's honor.

The book consists of four parts. The first describes some adventures of Telemachus and the suitors of Penelope. In the second part, Odysseus's time with Calypso is described, along with other adventures. Odysseus returns home in the third section, disguised as a beggar so that the suitors will not know who he is. He reveals himself to his son and his faithful servant Eumeus, then outlines his plans for revenge against the suitors. The last part describes his vengeance and his reunion with Penelope and his father Laertes.

Despite the engrossing storylines of these two epics, it was the heroic ideals that Homer conveyed that touched a national and cultural chord within Greeks everywhere. Listening to the brave deeds made Greeks all over the Aegean area see themselves in Homer's heroes and inspired them to carry on those ideals in their own city-states, which resulted in a newfound sense of commonality. And for that, Homer would become revered throughout all of Greece.

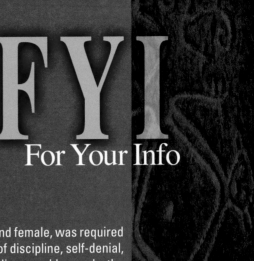

Spartan

Although Athens may be considered by many to be the greatest city-state because of its democratic ideals and pursuit of learning, there were nearly 1,500 other city-states scattered throughout the Aegean. Among these, Sparta was unique because of its dedication to producing the most competent and fierce army in the entire region.

To this end, every citizen of Sparta, both male and female, was required to be in perfect physical condition and to live a life of discipline, self-denial, and simplicity. When babies were born, Spartan soldiers would come by the house and check the baby. If the baby did not appear healthy and strong, the infant was taken away and left to die on a hillside. Sometimes the child was allowed to live but was trained as a slave, called a helot.

Young Spartan boys were sent away from home to military school when they were just six or seven years old. They were assigned to what was called a brotherhood. Members of the same brotherhood trained together and lived in the same barracks. Military school was often brutal, because being a great soldier meant being able to endure physical hardships, such as going hungry. They were also forced to march without shoes in order to toughen their feet. On the other hand, all the boys were taught to read and write as well.

When the boys were eighteen, they were required to pass a difficult test that measured their fitness, military ability, and leadership skills. Any Spartan males who failed were designated as perioikoi, or middle class. Perioikoi were allowed to own property and conduct business but were not citizens and had no political rights. But if they passed, they became full citizens and Spartan soldiers, and they would spend most of their lives with fellow Spartan soldiers. Even if they were married, Spartan soldiers did not live with their wives and families. Instead they continued to live in the barracks and train. If a Spartan soldier managed to live to be sixty years old, he could then retire from the military and move in with his family.

Spartan girls were also sent away to school when they were six or seven, and like the boys, they were required to live, sleep, and train in their sisterhood's barracks. Although the girls did learn some combat skills, they were also taught wrestling and gymnastics.

If a Spartan girl passed her test at eighteen, she was assigned a husband and allowed to return home. If she failed, she would lose her rights as a citizen and became a perioikoi. Interestingly, Spartan women had more rights than women in the other city-states. In most of Greece, women were required to stay inside their homes most of their lives, but in Sparta, female citizens enjoyed a great deal of freedom, probably since their husbands did not live at home.

Through his epic poems, Homer gave Ionians and Dorians alike a sense of individual and cultural pride. He is still revered today as one of the most important figures in Greek history.

CHAPTER
FIVE

HOMER'S LEGACY

After his visit to Athens, Homer eventually sailed to Ios, now called Ion, where he intended to spend some time. According to a translated text, Homer was relaxing while looking out over the sea when he asked some passing children if they had caught anything fishing. "All that we caught we left behind, and carry away all that we did not catch."[1]

Confused, Homer asked what they meant. They explained that they hadn't caught any fish but they had picked lice off their clothes, and they left the lice behind. However, all the lice they hadn't picked they brought with them in their clothes. By this time Homer was an old man. He remembered an old prophecy told to him by an oracle warning him that he would die on Ios after hearing a children's riddle. Convinced he didn't have long to live, Homer composed his own epitaph, then got up to leave. As he was walking away, he slipped and fell, suffering a critical injury. Three days later he died and was buried on Ios.

Homer died at the end of the Archaic period in Greece, which was the time that more and more people began preserving the past in writing. So his epics did not die with him. Scholars believe there were at least seven biographies of Homer written in the centuries after his death. Unfortunately, except for *The Life of Homer* credited to Herodotus, none of these biographies remain. However, we have been able to infer what little we do know about Homer from later existing references to these early texts.

Because Homer performed his epics in so many different places and in front of so many different people, there was a collective memory regarding the *Iliad* and *Odyssey*. At that time in history, people were trained to remember what they heard, so when the effort was made to put the epics down on paper—or papyrus, as the case may be—it would not have been surprising that people could transcribe them almost verbatim. Because epic poetry was performed orally, Homer would have been constantly tweaking the story, which would explain variations in style.

Professional singers called rhapsodes recited Homer's poetry throughout Italy and Greece, accompanying their performances with simple stringed instruments and teaching a new generation about Homer and his cast of heroes. It is believed that the earliest texts of *The Iliad* and *The Odyssey* were written certainly by 700 B.C., and more likely even earlier than that, from dictation by the Homeridae, rhapsodes who recited Homeric stories. By the time of Herodotus, the mid 400s B.C., Homer was already a legendary figure in Greece. Beyond that, other bards kept the stories alive through their own performances of the epics, which many people knew by heart. One reason it might have been easier for people to remember the verses is that there was a kind of formula used by epic poets. The storyteller would use phrases repeatedly to describe a person, place, or thing. For example, Achilles was described frequently as "of the swift feet" and

Apollo was the one "who strikes from afar." The repetition made remembering easier.

Looking at all the evidence, it seems Homer was recognized by the ancient Greeks as being the poet of *The Iliad* and *The Odyssey*. It wasn't until more modern times that scholars began expressing doubt over whether Homer indeed created both epics as we know them today or whether they are the work of multiple bards known collectively as Homer. Some scholars doubt that Homer ever really existed. The controversy was primarily caused by F. A. Wolf in his 1795 book *Prolegomena ad Homerum*, which questioned the authorship of *The Iliad* and *The Odyssey* and called into question the existence of Homer himself. It wasn't until the mid-nineteenth century that most scholars began to dismiss the arguments against Homer, and now most agree that the poet of *The Iliad*, with the Ionian name Homer, was a genuine historical person. In addition, most also agree that rather than merely being a "transmitter" of the epics, or someone who just amassed other people's stories, Homer played a direct part in creating these epics in the forms we know today. They credit him as not just a powerful artist but literary innovator as well. More to the point, if the Greeks and the Romans of the time were convinced that Homer was a single man and that he wrote the works that bear his name, why doubt it over two thousand years later?

Not only did *The Iliad* and *The Odyssey* provide great enter-tainment for audiences, the two epics also serve as a cultural and moral Grecian history, so much so that they have been likened to the Bible by some scholars. The stories are also considered masterpieces of Greek language. This is why in addition to being required reading in Greece, other cultures have also embraced the epics, including Italy, where Homer's poetry has been recited

Alexander the Great, King of Macedonia, conquered much of the then-civilized world and is considered one of the greatest generals in history. The Iliad, which recounted the story of Achilles during the Trojan War, was one of his favorite books.

and interpreted, criticized and studied. It is said that Alexander the Great, who was born in 356 B.C., so admired Achilles that he always kept a copy of *The Iliad* under his pillow.

At the end of his life, it appears Homer was aware of what his legacy and place in history might be. Before the fall that resulted in his death, he composed his own epitaph, which was later inscribed at his tomb. "Here the earth covers the sacred head of divine Homer, the glorifier of hero-men."[2]

Greek Heroes

In Greek mythology a hero was a famous individual who was worshiped almost as a god because of his deeds. Heroes were usually related to a god or divinity and often had special attributes. Below are some of the more famous heroes immortalized by Homer.

- Achilles (uh KIHL eez): The son of King Peleus and the sea nymph Thetis, he was dipped into the river Styx by his mother in order to make him invincible. She completely immersed him except for his heel where she held him. The bravest of the Greek heroes in the war against the Trojans, he was killed by an arrow to his heel, the only vulnerable part of his body.
- Aeneas (ih NEE uhs): Son of Venus and one of the few Trojan survivors of the fall of Troy. Virgil's epic *The Aeneid* tells his story after he escapes from Troy.
- Ajax (AY jacks): When the armor of Achilles was given to Odysseus, Ajax became jealous and planned to kill Odysseus in revenge. Realizing the evil inside him, Ajax killed himself.
- Diomedes (DIE oh mee deez): Along with Odysseus, Diomedes snuck into Troy and stole the Palladium, a statue of Athena said to be protecting the city. After the Trojan War he founded several Italian cities, including Brindisi.
- Evander (ee VAN der): In Roman mythology, Evander was an Arcadian hero of the Trojan War who founded the city of Pallantium near the spot where Rome was later built.
- Hector (HEC ter): Son of Priam, the Trojan hero Hector was killed by Achilles for accidentally killing Achilles' closest friend, Patroclus.
- Hercules (HUR kyuh leez): Son of Zeus and Alceme, Hercules was considered by many to be the greatest Greek hero, known for completing twelve difficult labors.
- Menelaus (mehn uh LAY uhs): King of Sparta, Menelaus was reunited with his wife, Helen, after the Trojan War.
- Odysseus (oh DIH see us): Greek leader during the Trojan War and creator of the wooden horse, Odysseus endured ten years of wandering before Poseidon allowed him to return home.
- Pericles (PEHR uh kleez): This Athenian statesman built Athens into a powerful empire.
- Perseus (PUR see uhs): Son of Zeus and Danae, Perseus killed Medusa, who was so fearsome that anyone who gazed upon her was turned to stone. Perseus conquered her by looking at her reflection in his shield and slaying her in her sleep.
- Priam (PRY uhm): Son of Laomedon and the nymph Strymo, Priam fathered fifty children, many by his wife, Hecuba. On the death of his father he became king of Troy.
- Theseus (THEE see uhs): Theseus was an Athenian who brought the natives of Attica together into the first democracy. He reportedly kidnapped Helen while she was very young, but she was rescued by her brothers while Theseus was visiting the underworld. Theseus also slew the Minotaur in its labyrinth on Crete with the help of Ariadne, who provided him with a sword and a roll of string so that he could find his way out.

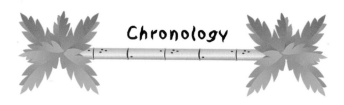

Chronology

c. 850 B.C. Melesigenes is born, most likely in Smyrna, to single mother, Critheis

- He and Critheis move in with her employer, Phemius

- Phemius marries Critheis, adopts Melesigenes and sends him to school

- Phemius dies and leaves school to Melesigenes

- Mother dies

- Melesigenes travels with Mentes

- While in Ithaca, is told story of Odysseus by Mentor

- Back in Smyrna, Melesigenes goes blind. Immerses himself in study of poetry

- Travels to Cyme where he begins performing poetry. He adopts the name Homer, local slang for a blind man

- Establishes a school in Chios and becomes successful teacher.

- Marries and has two children

- Starts traveling through Greece performing his epic poems

- Becomes the first to put his epics down in writing

- Dies on island of Ios

*Dates are unknown but relative to the times

BIOGRAPHY FROM
ANCIENT CIVILIZATIONS
LEGENDS, FOLKLORE, AND STORIES OF ANCIENT WORLDS

Timeline in History

1200 B.C.	Invention of steel; Trojan War begins
1193 B.C.	Greeks destroy Troy
1100 B.C.	Development of alphabetic script by the Phoenicians
800 B.C.	Beginning of Archaic Age
776 B.C.	First Olympic Games held
753 B.C.	Rome founded by Romulus
750 B.C.	Spread of Greek colonization throughout Mediterranean
700 B.C.	Homer and Hesiod composed their poems
650 B.C.	The rise of Greek lyric poetry
600 B.C.	Coin currency introduced.
563 B.C.	Buddha is born in India
551 B.C.	Confucius is born in China
537 B.C.	Beginnings of Greek drama
525 B.C.	Aeschylus, known as the father of Greek tragedy, is born at Eleusis
510 B.C.	Democracy begins in Athens
490 B.C.	Athens wins the Battle of Marathon
450 B.C.	Greek theater is at its height, and during this time many of its most famous plays are written
356 B.C.	Alexander the Great is born
146 B.C.	Rome defeats Greece, which becomes part of the Roman Empire

Chapter Notes

CHAPTER ONE

1. Leaf, Walter D., Schuchardt, K., Sellers, Eugenie. *Schliemann's Excavations: An Archeological and Historical Study*. Macmillan and Co., 1891 (London), p. 2.

2. James, H. R. *Our Hellenic Heritage. Volume: 1*. Macmillan & Co., 1921 (London), p. 110.

CHAPTER TWO

1. *The Life of Homer*, Herodotus.

2. Ibid.

CHAPTER THREE

1. *The Odyssey of Homer*. Translated by Alexander Pope. Heritage Press (New York), 1942. Reproduced on http://etext.library.adelaide.edu.au/h/h8op/h8op.html

2. Hesiod, *The Homeric Hymns and Homerica*. THE EPIGRAMS OF HOMER. Online Medieval and Classical Library. http://sunsite.berkeley.edu/OMACL/Hesiod/epigrams.html

CHAPTER FOUR

1. *The Iliad*, Homer. Translated by Samuel Butler. Book I. http://classics.mit.edu/Homer/iliad.html

CHAPTER FIVE

1. *Of the Origin of Homer and Hesiod and of their Contest*, translated by Hugh G. Evelyn-White, 1914.
http://sunsite.berkelev.edu/OMACL/Hesiod/homrhes.html and
http://www.sacred-texts.com/cla/homer/homrhes.htm

2. Ibid.

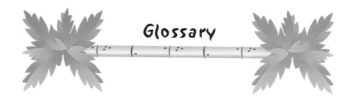

Glossary

Achaeans	(uh KEE uhnz) Another term for Ionians, or ancient Greeks.
Achilles	(uh KIHL eez) A Greek hero from Thessaly who is the main character in Homer's *Iliad*.
Aeneas	(ih NEE uhs) A Trojan prince who escaped from Troy after it had been sacked by the Greeks. According to legend his followers were the ancestors of the Romans.
Agora	(uh GORE uh) A large open space, usually situated in the center of a town, used for outside markets and public meetings. The psychological term *agoraphobia,* meaning "fear of public places," comes from this word.
Archaeologist	(are key AH luh jist) A scientist who learns about the past by unearthing and studying objects that have survived from former times.
Bronze Age	(bronz ayj) The period in human culture between the Stone Age and the Iron Age. It was marked by the use of bronze implements and weapons and lasted from about 3000 to 1100 B.C.
Chiton	(KY tuhn) The basic item of clothing for both men and women in ancient Greece. Chitons were made from a rectangle of fabric fastened at the shoulders and tied at the waist.
City-state	(SIH tee state) A small country controlled by a main, powerful city. Ancient Greece was made up of over one thousand city-states, the largest and most powerful of which were Athens, Sparta, and Corinth.
Classical Age	(CLASS ick uhl ayj) The period around 600 B.C. in Greece when arts and sciences flourished.
Democracy	(deh MAH creh see) A system of government in which citizens can vote to decide things. Athens had democracy from 510 B.C.
Dorians	(DAWR ee uhnz) A race of Greeks who supposedly invaded Greece from the north at the end of the Mycenean period (1400 to 1100 B.C.).

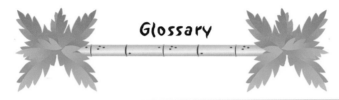

Glossary

Epic	(EH pic) A long narrative poem, such as *The Iliad,* that tells stories about heroic deeds. The first epics were presented orally and not written down.
Helot	(HEL ut) A Spartan slave, usually a native-born citizen deemed physically imperfect.
Hera	(HEER uh) Queen of the gods.
Heroes	(HEER ohs) Mortal men, often related to a god, who performed a particularly brave act in pursuit of honor and glory.
Himation	(hi MAT ee uhn) The outer cloak worn by ancient Greeks. This garment was traditionally worn with part of it pulled under the right arm and the other draped over the left shoulder.
Lyre	(lire) A stringed instrument popular in classical Greece.
Mount Olympus	(mount oh LIHM puhs) A mountain in Greece where the gods were thought to have lived.
Narrative	(NAIR uh tiv) A spoken story. An epic is a kind of narrative poem.
Odyssey	(OD uh see) Homer's *Odyssey* tells the story of what happens to the hero Odysseus during the ten years it takes him to get home after the end of the Trojan War. Now an odyssey has come to mean a long period of wandering or adventure.
Oracle	(AWR uh kuhl) A holy place where the gods could be asked questions with the help of a priest or priestess. The most famous oracle in ancient Greece was the Oracle of Apollo at Delphi.
Poseidon	(puh SY duhn) Greek god of the sea.
Prophecy	(PRAH fuh see) A foretelling of the future.
Sparta	(SPAR tuh) A powerful city in southern Greece famous for its soldiers, who were trained from birth.
Trireme	(TRY reem) The most widely used warship in ancient Greece; it was powered by three rows of oarsmen.
Troy	(troi) An ancient city on the coast of modern-day Turkey.
Zeus	(zoos) The most powerful of the ancient Greek gods.

For Further Reading

For Young Adults

Bloom, Harold. *Homer: Comprehensive Research and Study Guide.* New York: Chelsea House, 2001.

McCaughrean, Geraldine, and Victor G. Ambrus (illustrator). *The Odyssey.* Oxford: Oxford University Press, 1997.

McLaren, Clarence, and Joel P. Johnson. *Inside the Walls of Troy.* New York: Atheneum, 1966.

Picard, Barbara Leonie, and Joan Kiddell-Monroe (illustrator). *The Iliad of Homer (Oxford Myths and Legends).* Oxford: Oxford University Press Children's Books, 1991.

Sutcliff, Rosemary, and Alan Lee (illustrator). *Black Ships Before Troy: The Story of the Iliad.* New York: Delacorte Press, 1993.

Internet Addresses

Ancient Greece: History for Kids
http://www.historyforkids.org/learn/greeks/index.htm

BBC: Ancient Greece
http://www.bbc.co.uk/schools/ancientgreece/main_menu.shtml

Works Consulted

Adkins, Lesley, and Roy A. Adkins. *Handbook to Life in Ancient Greece.* New York: Facts on File, 1997.

Allan, Susan Heuck. *Finding the Walls of Troy: Frank Calvert & Heinrich Schliemann at Hisarlik.* Berkeley: University of California Press, 1998.

Burn, A. R., and Mary Burn. *The Living Past of Greece.* Boston: Little Brown and Company, 1980.

Herodotus. *History of Homer.* Translasted by Robin A. Waterfield. New York: Oxford University Press, 1998.

King, Wellington. *Heinrich Schliemann: Heros & Mythos.* University of Texas, http://www.utexas.edu/courses/wilson/ant304/biography/arybios97/kingbio.html, 1997.

Kivilo, Maarit. *The archaic biography of Homer.* http://www.ut.ee/klassik/sht/2001/kivilo2.pdf

Parsons, Jim; John Ewing; and Alex Newhart. *Greece: Discovering the Past.* Edmonton AB: Reidmore Books, 1992.

Payne, Robert. *The Gold of Troy: The Story of Heinrich Schliemann and the Buried Cities of Ancient Greece.* New York: Funk & Wagnalls Co., 1959.

Starr, Chester G. *The Ancient Greeks.* New York: Oxford University Press, 1971.

Traill, David A. *Schliemann of Troy: Treasure and Deceit.* New York: St. Martin's Press, 1995.

Heinrich Schliemann
http://emuseum.mnsu.edu/information/biography/pqrst schliemann_heinrich.html

Hesiod, the Homeric Hymns and Homerica. http://sunsite.berkeley.edu/OMACL/Hesiod/homrhes.html

Index